bound

bound

claire schwartz

for Zuzu. you teach me: love lives in the shape of a question.

for Ben. blood, i'd choose you every time.

～～

Published by Button Poetry / Exploding Pinecone Press

Minneapolis, MN 55403 | http://www.buttonpoetry.com

～～

Cover Design: Nikki Clark

ISBN 978-1-943735-28-0

...and I love
It, every drop of God
Weeping over me.

—JERICHO BROWN

Contents

behind the mechitza   1

for Mrs. Halachmi   2

looking at Chagall's "I and the Village" (1911)   4

distance is the primal fact   5

Geula Amir speaks   8

Birds   9

Self-Portrait with Lover and Country   10

Shards with Diffuse Light   11

someday, i'll love claire schwartz   16

& in the shards, smoke, & in the smoke, a message   17

When I Press My Spine to the Dirt & My One Fisted
Heart to the Open Ear of Night, I Can Hear It Rising Starward   18

looking at Chagall's "I and the Village" (1911)   23

the angel speaks to israel   24

Cross-Examination   25

invocation   26

████████   27

behind the mechitza

my mama tells me i have always loved women
who cover themselves, who shave their heads
and save their money until they can afford
human hair. say *eruv*, and i will hold you on my back,
say *back*, and i will see you hunched
beneath your negev. i have a hunch that the killers
are my cousins. you have been chosen
to carry the heaviest thing. does it matter
whose limbs i unzip from mine
in the morning so long as i have teeth to face
the day? my great-grandmother had a gummy smile
like you wouldn't believe. her belief was no joke.
my grandmother had a farm. she raised us.
she learned english, loved the word *sheep* best. i can hide
behind indefinite number. i hold all my mothers
in my chest. at night my ribs chatter
like the women in shul. try sleeping like that. i try
to count sheep, but they storm the fence.
the day i learned you can drown by drinking
too much water, i cried like i wanted
to make something grow in a desert. nobody knows
where negev comes from, it appears
to be part of a cluster of roots: *to make hollow,
to cut off, to dig*. there are so many hands
on my blood, my family, my killers for land—
sanguineous women, take my hand,
holy i will be, possessed as i am.

for Mrs. Halachmi

it's you on the other end saying, *come,*
come, and i hear the tongue flapping
beneath your tongue like a bird
crushed in a child's hand. we come,

packed in the small
and orange hour. pounds,
ovaries, appetite. you are falling
away from yourself slowly. you will not go

all at one time. i fall in love with time.
when you pull back from our embrace,
your hair clings to my hair

teacher, let me wear
your body through this life

these days, an elsewhere
pulls you close

how small and hinged these bones
how they prick and break
into a thousand stuttering wishes

the night is a fire
shot through with darkness,
the truth, an enduring
machine; it plods on. i am

i whom you named for your name.
you take my hand, you whisper to me.
on your vanishing tongue, a name
we have no thing for

looking at Chagall's "I and the Village" (1911)

Is it the sky or the cow's jowl? If the cow / has a human eye,
does that mean he knows something / about longing? If a man
walks toward his woman // with a sharp tool, do the rules
of gravity still apply? Can I call her / *his woman* if she doesn't
see him there // with his ordinary violence / and his labor? Can I call
her *his woman* if her woman / is waiting for her in the small
bluegreen house? How else // would you explain her
one-legged stance atop a house turned upside down? If you can
believe / in gravity, how can you not believe / that the beautiful one
with a belly full of comets is in that house—just now / peeling back
the sheets / and lying down to wait? Will you look again? // Don't
you see that switch of hips? Don't you see / that purple swagger?
How could that be other // than the dance of a woman in love? Who
is that man / whose whole house is window? Do you think he envies
the women? Do you / think he regrets the stormy days? Is there //
weather here? What is burning? Why is the house red? The crusty /
earth? The man's hat? Why are even his wide green
face // and the blue of the sky so, so red?

distance is the primal fact

all day i make myself small
and wait to come home to the only woman
i let close enough to hurt
when i retract from her touch.
at the dinner she has made for us i continue
not to eat, press words like *bungalow*
and *ethereal* against my cheek's soft meat,
consider writing a dictionary
that catalogs words according to the pleasures
they give my mouth. i say, *listless*
sounds like the inability to catalog
and listen as the steak cools. i think
about making a record called *the stink*
of distance. i wear all my clothes to bed.
when she reaches for me, i make my body
into a fist. somewhere a womb
is opening to take me in. the origins are brutal
and full of liquid. six years ago, i am at mt. sinai,
a hospital where there are brochures and men
with certificates and hands that have been washed. now
the things inside of me are sterile. i crave the desert
lodged beneath my fingernails, the honest sun
that pulls back my skin. no, i don't resent moses
his golden calf. there are days i light myself on fire
just to worship something glittering. all the light
here has passed through a chemical bath
and the promise of reason. i have yet to see a poet
smuggle *rape kit* into a stanza and make it sing.
my lover's body is a metronome. i listen

as sleep portions her breath
into something even, perfect.
once again, i am held
on the outside of time.

in the dream, it's not the doctor
but the blond and wispy social
worker. say *ahhhhh,* she directs me. i say
nothing, but stick my tongue out as she lays down
the depressor and then, carefully, a tiny
potted plant. *you're all set,* she says cheerfully,
as i think about how i once saw a man
slumped against the wall of a subway station
gagging while no one, especially me,
helped him. i think about how i am
especially me and gag. all day,
i walk around with my tongue
out just so. my mouth's roof becomes moist then wet
then a torrential downpour. the potted plant
blooms. years pass in my mouth. seeds,
new plants, vines, flowers, mulch, rot.
my mouth is a jungle. outside, it is evening.
i am sitting on a stoop on 104th street,
my tongue aching under this whole and florid world.
the social worker walks out of a bakery with coffee
and two scones and i think she must have a lover
or an appetite. she stops to look at my tongue
overgrown with foliage. *you should have said,* ahhhhh. *you
should have said anything.*

i wake, this terrible and once-again-miracle
of morning. my lover is a still-warm imprint
on the left side of our bed. she is not yet on a plane
bulleting across the sky in all directions
not toward me. desire is an imprecise vector.
i find her in the kitchen. all across america
lovers are looking at their lovers' backs
and wondering what comes next. mine pours
the coffee. we watch the steam rise, then go to a place
from which it can never be called back

Geula Amir speaks

again with the american journalists
who come to call
my sons *murderers,* again
with my sons who rise redly
waving their four good hands
like their best name has been spoken
by the wide blue mouth of their god
or prime minister, O,
when a child dies, the village keens,
when children kill, there is only one mother
to kneel & lap the blood
from their names,
O forked & feral tongue,
i spit in the tea & carry the cup
to the journalist perched on the couch
i cleaned just this morning, whose bald head
shines like something polished, O stupid sun,
O futile gesture, smokestack, yeshiva, fanatic
in one hundred languages, O headlines,
bylines, ball bearings, rigged & riddled,
O new & no speech of mine,
when i die, who will be there
to write the end of history?

Birds

The day my grandmother fled her homeland, a thousand birds
blackened the sky like night. That's not true, but I never know

what to say to call you close. In their 1676 volume *Ornithologiae*,
Francis Willughby and John Ray developed the first classification

of birds. Oh, bird. What will I do with you? Everything
I write, a way of saying: *Look what I can do*

with language. I am trying to tell you: *I miss wonder*. I wonder
if nostalgia is what we invented to name ourselves *species*

and mean: *we once stood on the same shore*. If history
were as brackish as what thrashes in us, how could we possibly

worship our reflections? Show me an animal who has built a god
from such roiling waters. In my house, a stiller mirror. Some say glass

is liquid moving very, very slowly. Speed it up and, there,
the ocean, like the one my grandmother watched

the birds dive into—headfirst, all at once. Once, a woman fell in love
with a bird. She spent her whole life removing power lines

and painting glass doors. Stay with me. I just want us to see
what we are crashing into. In 1758, Carl Linneas modified

Ornithologiae to devise the taxonomic system currently in place.
Classification is a country. If the pens of white men had fallen

differently, we might share a homeland. I might be a bird.

Self-Portrait with Lover and Country

Like any good American, I am holding a pillow over History's mouth
while I guide your hand past my waistband. Like any good woman,
History finds a trapdoor. In your bed, it gets heated. I open
the window and white women are crying out—
a monster bride with a cop holding her
train. I sing to them and call it *comfort*. I love the track
on your wrist my waistband leaves. I am forever shredding joy
trying to make things stay. Where has History gone? There she is,
in the armchair in the corner, smoking a cigarette, tapping
the butt with her long forefinger. The floor flickers
orange. On your clock, the minutes glow green. We buy one
and climb inside. You pass me syllables of softness
sifted from the wreck of your boyhood. We write sentences of salt
and skin. *You're hurting me,* one of us says to the other.
One of us laughs. Here I am, trying to crush History
with my bare hands. Here you are, pinning my hands
above my head. No one told me about this particular pleasure. You
once told me other planets are hospitable to life. Before boarding a
spaceship, I want to know: where is the god who refuses
to turn a woman to salt? *Don't look back,* History cackles,
crushing ash under the toe of her boot. I wish she would just stop
laughing. I wish she would just stop. She can't contain herself.
*Can you believe it? I carved a moral from this ruin
and sold it to a tourist.* She is closer now. I can feel her
hot breath on the back of my neck. One of us screams.
One of us looks away.

Shards with Diffuse Light

In the dream, the oldest woman—

Knees & knees & elbows. All that creaking makes a door.
Pass over it.

Once, my people ensured safety by marking our doorposts
with the blood of a lamb. Every year, we tell the story.

When I say, safety, I mean: *We were spared.* When I say, *We,*
I mean: *not counting the ones not spared.*

It's true. I still believe
my people.

The oldest woman spits three times. From the sand: marigolds.

I say, *In the dream* to temper what I conceived in full waking.
Even here, I am hiding. In my pocket, a spare name.

Most of the soft country of my brain is uninhabited.

Despite the song I learned as a child, Palestine
was very much inhabited in 1948.

In 2002, in order to practice staging military assaults, the Israeli
Defense Force *started to upgrade a small mock-up town located
at the IDF's base of Tze'elim in the Negev desert, named Chicago
(invoking the bullet-ridden myth of the American city).*

Dear Almost Was—

Roger Fisher wanted to bring nuclear war out of the realm
of abstraction. His suggestion: *Put that needed code in a little*
capsule, and then implant that capsule in the heart of a volunteer.

In Chicago, I fell in love.

The volunteer would carry with him a big, heavy butcher knife
as he accompanied the President. If ever the President wanted to fire
nuclear weapons, the only way he could do so would be for him first,
with his own hands, to kill one human being. He has to look
at someone and realize what death is.

Every 20 seconds, someone looks at someone, then kills them.

We lay in your bed. You picked up the big, heavy
butcher knife. In the capsule in my heart: beaks, a ball of fur, twine,
a silk patch (blue), Prazosin (45 mg), a clot of hair.

I am forever disappointing you.

I am always making your body into a door.

Tell me a story of two bodies not threaded with violence.

Between 1948 & 1954, Israeli officials told hundreds of Mizrahi
parents—most from Yemen—that their newborns or young children
had died. Really, they were kidnapped & sold to Ashkenazi families.
I did not learn this in Hebrew school.

It's true. I love the dead best.

Once, I found a tooth in the dirt. I put it in my mouth.

White people go to protests & ask police for directions home.

I am implicated. Now what?

If, right now, you lay down this poem & walk off with all your eyes
& tongues—yes.

Please, stay.

Dear Littlest— Dear Not Yet—

Who counts
you?

At night, I dress in silt. This way I am closer to my grandmother.

In this version, the minute is hollowed. We enter it—& live.

When I say, *We,* I mean: *everyone who hauls their dead
up the mountain called* day.

10:57 a.m.—imminent nuclear war with little persistences. Eyebrow
threading. Milk marbling coffee. Imposter syndrome. Ants.

At my prettiest, I am my state's most terrible ornament.

Nearly all of the Mizrahi parents whose children had supposedly died were given a recruitment order from the IDF when their supposedly dead children were approaching the age of recruitment.

I have a truth & a family—which do I serve?

The last time I went to Bethlehem, I was the same age as the IDF soldiers checking ids. *Schwartz. American.* I passed easily. *What are you doing here?* is a question I was not asked but should always ask myself.

Everyone who raised me has a string of numbers tattooed on their forearm. Or the ghost of a string of numbers.

Last night, a man whose name I'll never know said, *call me*
[   ]. I call & call & call

Swallow. I am told that makes you a woman.

Morning, & I am still disappointing. I take the big, heavy butcher knife, cut from my throat to my belly button. Part the reddest sea. From my chest, an exodus: all of my mothers. Single-file & singing. Forearms clean canvases of skin. Marigolds braided into their hair.

I am always showing you my scars & hoarding my wettest wounds.

I am scared to stop
hurting. Is there another route
back to you?

At night, I unstitch : an ancient song

How red the making of white women.

On the bus, everyone has a spine so tender it once had to be held up by the hand of a person whose spine had already hardened.

There is nothing between my forefinger & this stranger's ear. How vulnerable.

Despite it all: tenderness.

Do you think I didn't see you? you asked as you were leaving. I think you saw me completely, & left anyway.

Love is so embarrassing.

I bled in your bed. I'm sorry.

I have built you a shore with all my best words & still, the waves.

someday i'll love claire schwartz

after Ocean Vuong / after Roger Reeves / after Frank O'Hara

claire, close your eyes. try to see. every woman
you've ever loved has been inlaid with scales

& ash. here are the matches. gather some tinder. strike
your teeth until they spark. you can still hear her name

on your tongue, clean as the sound the axe makes, then muffled
like the year between you is a closed door. listen closely. even you

can whittle your selves into something another can use
for heat. claire, be brave. your people will be back

with their stamping & their songs. they will build you
a birthright, then tell you to hold it with all your limbs

& veins. look for the blood beneath the story. when they say *land,*
reply: *history.* to *tribe: history.* to *song: behold this symphony*

of synapses. every day goes right enough to pin this animal body
to earth a little longer. remember the cat who brought you exquisite

gift of corpse after corpse. you should be so lovely.
one day you will lay down this body & walk off

into the night with only the wind whistling
your human name & a mouthful of language

seeking a mouth

& in the shards, smoke,
& in the smoke, a message

faygele,   i will grow up
to be your house
& when they come
to burn me down,   i will grow
up to be a city of ashes
& angels where all the houses
have flags,   & all the flags
have your face

When I Press My Spine to the Dirt & My One Fisted Heart to the Open Ear of Night, I Can Hear It Rising Starward

Photograph:
Jakob Glatstein with the Children's Choir in the Warsaw Ghetto

Caption:
"The children's hair was shaved because of lice."

Not Nazi orders, but the hunger of tiny insects
who took six-legged hold & sucked something sweet
from them who were hungry, made meat
of them who had not mother nor president,
& upon their heads: razors & women
who worked their scalps
so raw it was like creation
in reverse. (Is there anything more
mother?) Ode to the hair
& how it tumbled like fruit
dropped by the hand of a tree
to the earth, where it would not be
braided by the long fingers of sisters
who kept to themselves
all of their bones for as long
as they possibly could. Ode to the body
which is not a tree, but which sometimes makes
of itself shade & fruit. Ode to, again, the hair,
how it piled like the shorn eyelashes

of people & giants, a tribe
whose members circled & said to each other,
Ready yourself to watch, or else, *We have seen
enough.* Ode to the little girl who ran past
the bodies strewn in the street, flapping her arms
like she was trying to churn wind
into something she could hold
or eat. Ode to running, how the whole body becomes
heart, stubborn muscle wanting
only to keep on, keep, on, & then,
to stop. (The heart is not a fist
though they are the same size & both stashed
with longing.) Ode to the girl who took her place
in the third row, who, when the photographer
said, *Smile,* smiled wide like she had no idea
what was to come. & Jakob Glatstein, teacher,
owed, who every morning in the ghetto awoke,
put on his glasses, saw their galloping hearts
& red mouths, Jakob Glatstein,
who said, *Sing.* Who said, *Yes,
take our picture.*

I see them in Jerusalem
at Yad Vashem, framed
& flat, where the names
stack on stones that say
to some, *We will never
forget,* to others, *You will not
grow here.* I was not raised
on this land though I have birthright,
I am told, to bikini

& grenade. In the museum,
everyone has a heart quickened
with desire & a history
distended with myth.

Once, clutching his deportation papers,
my grandfather's cousin
told me the story of his first kiss
within the ghetto walls. This
is not about the ghetto walls.
This is about how the stomach shimmies
then plummets like a baby bird
pushed from the nest
when that beautiful child
finds some other beautiful
child he wants to lay in the barn with
& say, "Look at this spider,
her eight & spindle legs,
how quietly she writes herself
into home, how her webbed language glitters
when you lay on your back
just here at just this hour. I noticed this
for you." Which is another way of saying: "You
grew me these better eyes, thank you."
Jakob Glatstein & the children of the Children's
Choir in the Warsaw Ghetto, thank you
for these eyes. Which is to say: I have fallen
in love with you.

Can't you see now
what I've been trying
to tell you, how I've been

trying to make of this poem
an unbombed-out home, but a poem
has no walls, only a thousand tiny mouths
with all their percussive teeth & tongues
doing all that tongues will—
one & then all of them singing an ode
to Ahmad Sharaka, 13-years-old,
who is, in this poem, not yet
killed by IDF bullets knuckling his ribs, who is,
just now, clutching the flag of Palestine
in his chest, his arm stretching back
like an angel's silver wing
& in his hand, a stone
which he throws at the tank
lumbering down his streets,
which it hits with the smallest
song, a tuning fork, keying us in
to this song I am trying now to sing
with all the angels & children
& with you, this song
which is, after all, an ode
to streets which are not now
home to playgrounds or children
joyously tearing free of their fathers'
hands, but Ahmad
has hands, two, & he gives them
sometimes to his mother
when she comes home from the souk making
of her arms a basket
piled high with olives & with grain

& here in this poem is a smaller poem
where that boy tugs at his mother's shirt & she turns
& spoons some coffee into a small blue cup
& they sit outside together, unafraid,
dressing the night with their laughter & their quiet

Come, strangerlove, be with me this evening
I will make the coffee how you like it,
just a little bit sweet. Lay down
your whole body where you are
on this good earth, & tell me: can you see it
climbing up into the sky? The children
of the Warsaw Ghetto & their teacher
& my grandfather & the stone & the beautiful
boy who threw it, like, no, not smoke,
but a single, shimmering note

looking at Chagall's "I and the Village" (1911)

slaughterslaughterslaughterslaughterslaughterslaughters
laughterslaughterslaughterslaughterslaughterslaughtersl
aughterslaughterslaughterslaughterslaughterslaughtersla
ughterslaughterslaughterslaughterslaughterslaughterslau
ghterslaughterslaughterslaughterslaughterslaughterslaug
hterslaughterslaughterslaughterslaughterslaughterslaugh
terslaughterslaughterslaughterslaughterslaughterslaught
erslaughterslaughterslaughterslaughterslaughterslaughte
rslaughterslaughterslaughterslaughterslaughterslaughter

the angel speaks to israel

an old man & boy walk along the bank
of the crooked river you named
for my face (knowing nothing more
than to call it *face*) after the night
i touched your hip & you begged

for my name. the mute woman with her head
out the window at twilight is my mother.
i had no name. i gave you a new name
& slipped yours on my closest self
so in the depths of memory,
you might summon me. i want you close

& ineffable, like a lover who clings
to what his lover's scent clings to.
i have no scent. how lonely to long
without the body's promise
of betrayal. how gorgeous, how human, the kiss
after night bakes breath into something unsavory.

in the water, from heaven,
this smallest mirror, i see my face & call out,
jacob. the old man wades. my speaking lips
ripple. the boy plunges in. froth consumes my face.

israel, the messenger is myth. there is no body
untransformed under another's desire.

Cross-Examination

What is poetry which does not save
Nations or people?
–Czesław Miłosz

what is a country but the drawing of a line
–Safia Elhillo

What is a nation which does not save
poetry? What is a poem but the gathering
of lines? What is a line but people
waiting? What is waiting but satisfaction
suspended? What is a break but a suspension
of breath? What is breath when the body
is broken? What is a line break but hunger
with no mouth? What is a nation where
no one is hungry? What is hunger but people
wanting? What is a line but desire given form?
What is a people but a form of survival? What
is a form without an outside? What is a country
without an other? What is a poem but a gesture
of reaching? Can a poem save a nation? Can a poem
survive a nation? Can a poem survive a savior? Can
a poem feed a people? Can a body survive
a people? What do you call a body bent in labor? Who
is this poem working for? What is a poem that leaves
people hungry? What is a poem that leaves people
wanting? When wanting takes leave, where
is the question? How can a poem be
when there is no question?

invocation

god of moss
god of katydids and walnut husks
god of the sky darkened with pigeons
god of the sky darkened with night

Israeli Prime Minister Benjamin Netanyahu spoke before a joint session of Congress on March 3, 2015. Here are his full remarks.

(Associated Press)

NETANYAHU: ████████████████

████████████████

████████████████

████████████████

██
██
██
██████████████████████████████████

I ███ want ██████████████████████████████████████
████████████████ to see ████████████ your feet.

████████████████

I guess it's true what they say ████████████████████████████
████████████

████████████████

████████████████ I'm deeply humbled by the ████████████████████
████████████████████████████████████ body ██
████████████████████████████████████

(APPLAUSE)

██
██ I ██████
regret ███████████████ my being here ████████████ That was
never my intention.

I want to thank ████████████████████████████████████
██
████████

████████████████

██
████████████████████████

████████████████

██ destiny ██████
██ and ██████
hope ██
████████████ and ███ America's presidents ████████████████
████████████████████████████

████████████████████

████████████████████████████ President Obama ████████████████████

████████████████████ is ████████████████

████████████████

██
████████████████

██████████████████████████████████ fire| and
█████████████████████████████████████

aid.

██████████████████████████████ again,
he provided vital ████████████████████████

████████████████████████████████
███████████████████████████ terrorists.

████████████

███████████████████ I called ██████████ and he was
██████

███████████████████████████████
██████████████████████████ the most
sensitive █████████████████████████████
███████████████████████████

████████████████████████████████
████████████████████████████████
██████████████ missile defense██████████
██████████

(APPLAUSE)

████████████████████████████████
████████████████ this capital dome helped
build our Iron Dome.

(APPLAUSE)

Thank you, America. Thank you for everything you've done
██████████

My friends, ████████████████████████████████████
████ I feel a profound obligation to ██████████████
████████████ threaten ████████████████████
████████████ Iran ████████████

██
██
██
████████████████████████████████████
██
████████████████████████████████████
██
██
██

The plot was foiled. ██████████████████

██████████████

██
██
Ayatollah Khamenei ██████████████████████
██
██████████████████████████ tweets in
English ████████████████████████

██
██
██
██████████████ save us ████████████████
██████████████████████

the entire

brutal dictatorship

drafted a constitution

goons   lackeys   revolutionary
guards   with three
tentacles
                 are

█████████████████████████████████████

███████████████████████████ all too real.

████████████ America ████████████████████
██
████████████████████████████████████
███████████████████████████████

██
████████████████████████ blew up █████████
██
██
██
Washington, D.C.

██
██
██

██████████████████████████████████ the
community of nations ████ is busy gobbling up the nations.

(APPLAUSE)

██
██████████████ terror.

(APPLAUSE)

███████████████████████████████████████
███████████████████████████████████████
██████████████████████████████████

████████████████████████ gays ██████████████████
██████████████████████████████████

████████████████████████████ charm █ Western diplomats ███
██████████ at the grave of Imad Mughniyeh.
███████████████████████████████████████
██████████████████████████████ I'd like to
see someone ask ████ a question about that.

███████████████████████████████████████
███████████████████████████████████████
█████████████████

███████████████████████████████████████
███████████████████████████████████████
███████████████████████████████████████
███████████

Don't be fooled. ████ battle ██████████████████████ doesn't
turn ████████████████████████████

███████████████████████████████████████
████████████████████████████████████
██████████████████████████████████
███████████████████████████████████████
███████████████████████████████████
█████████████

women

to

butcher knives

and YouTube

We must always remember   time

explain why
certain elements   are now a
     public
secret   You can Google it.

break out

the bomb. Break out the

bomb.

According to a single

spinning

program
break-out time would be very short

True, certain restrictions would be

the
problem inspectors

cameras,

locks

Now, I know

you

could be hiding

in the life of our children. We all have a responsibility to consider

enriching uranium.

The foremost sponsor
of global terrorism could be

my friend

That's
why this deal is so

bomb.

I believe

in

a

wet appetite

Would I be

gobbling up four

countries

And

████████ nuclear tripwires ████████████████████████

██

If anyone thinks – ████████████████████████████████
████████████████ think again.

██

██

████████████

██

██

██

████████████████████████████████

██

██

████████████████████████

(APPLAUSE)

██

██

████████████████████████████████

(APPLAUSE)

██

(APPLAUSE)

████████████ stop threatening to annihilate my ████████

████████████████████████████

████████████

powers

If ▮▮▮▮▮▮▮▮▮▮▮ the restriction ▮▮▮▮▮▮▮ doesn't change its behavior, the restrictions should not be ▮▮▮▮▮

▮▮▮▮▮▮▮▮▮▮ treated like ▮ normal ▮▮▮▮ let it act ▮▮ , normal ▮▮▮▮

My friends, what about ▮▮▮▮▮▮▮▮▮▮▮▮▮▮

the price of oil

(APPLAUSE)

you have the power to make

a bad deal. a very bad deal. We're better off without

the alternative That's just

a much better deal.

█████████████████

█████████

███████████████████████████
███████████████████████████
██████████████████████

█████████

███████████████████████████
███████████████████████████
████████

Ladies and gentlemen, history has placed us at a fateful crossroads. We must now ███████████████████ ████████████████████████████████ inexorably ████████████ ██████████████████████████████████ lead to war.

███████████████████████████
███████████████████████████
███████████████████████████
█████████

You don't have to read Robert Frost to know ████████████ ███████████████████████████ ███████████████████████████ ███████████████████████████ ████████████████████

█████████

standing up to Iran is not easy. ███████

███████████████████████████████████████

███████████████████████████████

███████████████

███████████████████████████████████

██████████████████

████████████

███████████████████████████████████

███████████████████████████████████

████████████████████████████

██████████████

███████████████████████████████████

████████████████████████████

But I can guarantee you this, █████████████████

███████████████████████████████████

████████████████████

████████████

We are no longer ███████████████████████████

███████████████████████████████████

███████████████████████████████████ the Jewish
people, ██████████████████████

███████████████

This is why ████████████████████████
████████████████████████████ Israel has to stand alone,
████████████████

(APPLAUSE)

But I know that Israel does not stand ██████████████
America stands ████████████

████████████

████████████ you stand ████████████

████████████

████████████████████████████ you ██████████████
██████████████████████████████████████
████████████████████████ succumb to
████████████████

████████████

██████████████████████████████████
████████████████████████ the image ██████████
████████████████████████ of the Promised Land.

██████████████████████████████████
Moses gave us a message ████████████████████████
██████████████████████████████████
██████████████████████████████████
████████████████

██████████████████████████████████
██████████████████████████████████

█████████ May we face the ██████████████████
████████████████

██ God ██████████████████████████████
████████████ of America.

(APPLAUSE)

Thank you. Thank you very much. Thank you all.

You're ████████████

████████████America. Thank you.

Thank you.

notes

"for Mrs. Halachmi" is in memory of Miriam Halachmi (b. 1944, Binyamina, Israel; d. 2015, Nashville, TN).

"distance is the primal fact" takes its title from the first line of James Galvin's "Three Sonnets."

"Geula Amir speaks": Geula Amir is the mother of Yigal and Hagai Amir, right-wing Jewish brothers and conspirators who assassinated Israeli Prime Minister Rabin. Although the brothers take outspoken pride and responsibility for the well-documented assassination, a third of Israelis, including their mother, do not believe they are guilty.

In the summer of 2017, Hanif Abdurraqib visited the Kenyon Young Writers Program. Asked his advice for young writers, he said: "If you have birds in your poem, tell us what kinds. Don't just say 'birds.'" From that advice: "Birds." It is dedicated to Hanif Abdurraqib.

The quotations in "Shards with Diffuse Light" are from Eyal Weizman's *Hollow Land: Israel's Architecture of Occupation* (2007) and Roger Fisher's "Preventing Nuclear War," published in the *Bulletin of Atomic Scientists* (1981). The poem's form holds in mind the kabbalistic belief שבירת הכלים, which refers to the shattering of the vessels into which divine light was poured during Creation.

gratitude

to the editors of the following publications in which these poems, sometimes in earlier versions, first appeared:

Tupelo Quarterly: "behind the mechitza" | *Prairie Schooner*: "for Mrs. Halachmi" and "distance is the primal fact" | *Tongue*: "Birds" | *Beloit Poetry Journal*: "Geula Amir speaks" | ButtonPoetry.tumblr.com: "& in the shards, smoke, and in the smoke, a message" | *Waxwing*: "someday i'll love claire schwartz" | *Bennington Review*: "Cross-Examination" | *A Portrait in Blues: An anthology of identity, of gender, of bodies* (Platypus Press): "Self-Portrait with Lover and Country" | *The Massachusetts Review*: "█████████"

~~~

Sam, Nikki & Hanif & the rest of the Button team. patient seers. thank you for claiming me.

Aziza Barnes. your *yes* bound these poems. thank you.
Yale African American Studies & American Studies//Jacqueline Goldsby. Kobena Mercer. Lisa Monroe. Anthony Reed.
Jodie Stewart-Moore. Anusha Alles, Danielle Bainbridge, Nick Forster, Lauren Meyer, Maryam Parhizkar, Tina Post || Williams College//Lillian-Yvonne Bertram. Joyce Foster. Wendy Raymond. Vince Schleitwiler. Dorothy Wang. Leslie Wingard.

by hug & example & well-worked line: Aracelis Girmay, Cornelius Eady, Robin Coste Lewis, Kevin Quashie, Claudia Rankine, Evie Shockley.

teachers of my life: Elizabeth Alexander, Miriam Halachmi, Stéphane Robolin. thank you.

& students, who teach me.

thank you, too:

K. Tajhi Claybren. what love you make possible with your loving.
Tony Coleman. mural-hearted love, tuesday-poemed promise.
Michaiah Coleman. you sew the wild possibilities of new words. i can't wait to keep knowing you.
Shayla Fender. you move toward what matters, always, with love enough to hold this world.
Annie Joseph-Gabriel. you carry your genius like a lantern.
Melissa Gordon. you poem me, always. i hope you know.
Efe Igor. question-seeker, beauty-sharer, bringer of radiance.
Bridget Ngcobo. you gracious, you perfect, you ocean-stretched love. Noah Remnick. brother to my other brother, brother to me.
Jessica Schwartz. the growth of your questions & commitments has moved my whole life.
Sophie & Laura & Izzy Solomon. you dangling earrings & open doors.

Emily Chu. these poems would not be these poems without your heart & your pen. your always, your steadfast. your pasta, your purple. on a street in Claremont, the lyrics are whatever we sing loudest. you build summer in every season.

my beautiful & scattered blood. grandparents—for the bravery of before & the possibilities of alongside. aunts & uncles, who parent me. & cousins & cousins. & parents, especially. what winged roots are these.

reader. every word seeks to deserve you.

About the Author

Claire Schwartz's poetry has appeared in Apogee, Beloit Poetry Journal, The Massachusetts Review, and Prairie Schooner, and her essays, reviews, and interviews in The Iowa Review, Los Angeles Review of Books, Virginia Quarterly Review, and elsewhere. She is a PhD candidate in African American Studies and American Studies at Yale.

Other Books by Button Poetry

If you enjoyed this book, please consider checking out some of our others, below. Readers like you allow us to keep broadcasting and publishing. Thank you!

Aziza Barnes, *me Aunt Jemima and the nailgun.*
J. Scott Brownlee, *Highway or Belief*
Nate Marshall, *Blood Percussion*
Sam Sax, *A Guide to Undressing Your Monsters*
Mahogany L. Browne, *smudge*
Neil Hilborn, *Our Numbered Days*
Sierra DeMulder, *We Slept Here*
Danez Smith, *black movie*
Cameron Awkward-Rich, *Transit*
Jacqui Germain, *When the Ghosts Come Ashore*
Hanif Willis-Abdurraqib, *The Crown Ain't Worth Much*
Aaron Coleman, *St. Trigger*
Olivia Gatwood, *New American Best Friend*
Donte Collins, *Autopsy*
Melissa Lozada-Oliva, *Peluda*
William Evans, *Still Can't Do My Daughter's Hair*
Rudy Francisco, *Helium*

Available at buttonpoetry.com/shop and more!